With best wishes

B Rourke

WHEN YOU WERE

WEE

BY SPECIAL REQUEST

THE CHILDHOOD MEMORIES OF
CECIL BROOKE MULLAN

authorHOUSE®

AuthorHouse™ UK Ltd.
500 Avebury Boulevard
Central Milton Keynes, MK9 2BE
www.authorhouse.co.uk
Phone: 08001974150

First published by AuthorHouse 6/17/2009

ISBN: 978-1-4389-9448-2 (sc)

This book is printed on acid-free paper.

THIS BOOK
IS WRITTEN FOR
AND
DEDICATED TO

my two wonderful
granddaughters

Alexandra Brooke

&

Faye Annabelle

Acknowledgements & Thanks

I wish to thank my wife Beryl, my family and the many close friends who encouraged me to put some of my stories into writing.

My thanks too to Abie Greyvenstein for his excellent illustrations which help bring the book to life.

And special thanks are due to Caroline Haywood at Authorhouse Publications, for her most valued help and advice in guiding me through the preparation of this my 'first' book

But most important of all, I thank God, under whose protection and care I was permitted to travel and enjoy these wonderful and amazing adventures at such an early age, the kind that most little boys might only dream of.

Contents

Introduction

Dear Alex and Faye,

I have written down these stories for you in response to your repeated request:

"tell us stories, Grandpa, about when you were wee"

and it has been a great pleasure for me to do it because of the wonderful memories I have of you, Alex, sitting on my left knee, and you Faye, on my right; it seemed that for one reason or another these were always your chosen positions.

As you read them now, I hope that they will   bring you just as   much enjoyment and amusement as they did when I first told them to you. I think I have them more or less in the order that they happened but in some places I might just have remembered something and put it in.

Grandpa

Chapter 1 – Where did granny go?

When I was born on the 5th April 1944 the second world war was still on and we lived with my granny in Belfast.

She was a quiet little woman but became very nervous when the sirens sounded – these were to warn people that German bombers were coming over our city.

If it was at night time you had to make sure that none of the lights in the house could be seen from the sky, so curtains always had to be closed very tightly.

Some people went into underground garden shelters through a flat door or a hatch.

Granny Moore used to hide under the kitchen table and we all thought it very funny.

Of course, I was only wee, and I guess I don't *really* remember that bit.

Someone probably told me.

Still, it's very funny every time I think about it.

Chapter 2 – Water water everywhere

But what I really wanted to tell you is that when I was four years old my Mum and Dad and my wee sister and I all left Belfast and got on a big ship down at the docks.   It was called the Liverpool Boat.

Uncle Joe was Aunt Jean's husband (he used to be in the Air Force and had a very nice moustache). Aunt Jean said she loved kissing a man with a moustache because it tickled; and he looked really handsome in his smart uniform as well .

I remember seeing a photograph of him in Aunt Jean's house. Aunt Jean liked men in uniforms.

Well, what I was going to say is that he went with us on the boat to Liverpool. You see, none of us had ever been out of Ireland before and because he was from England he knew his way around.

I can't remember it but Uncle Joe told me that I went all over the ship turning on all the taps I could find so that there was water running everywhere. It's funny when I think about it now, because whenever I do anything with water, I seem to get it everywhere.

Nana says that when I do the dishes the whole floor is soaking wet.

Another thing Uncle Joe told me was that when he and Aunt Jean used to take me into town I always put one shoe on top of the other one when I was standing and scuffed the good white shoes that they had bought for me.

Chapter 3 – down the drain

Oh! I forgot to tell you – one day when we were still living in Belfast, Aunt Jean's engagement ring got lost.

Everyone was looking for it everywhere but they just couldn't find it. Then someone said, "Maybe we should ask Brooke", and so my Mum came and asked me if I knew where Aunt Jean's ring was. I was three at the time.

Of course I did; and leading them all out into what was called *'the back yard'* I pointed to the drain just below the kitchen window and said "down there".

They took off the cover and lo and behold glittering there in the sunlight was Aunt Jean's ring.

... and I didn't even get scolded!

Chapter 4 – The flying highchair

Well, back to Liverpool and Uncle Joe took us to the big ship that was to carry us across the Atlantic Ocean to Canada. The ship's name was 'Arcadia' and because the captain knew that it was going to be a very rough crossing and that conditions might not be very good, he made my Dad sign a piece of paper promising that he would not complain about anything during the voyage.

One very stormy morning I was sitting

in my highchair having breakfast with my Dad – my Mum and my wee sister didn't feel like eating anything.

Suddenly a big wave hit the side of the ship and all the cups and saucers and plates started flying everywhere and they had to put sides up on the tables so that our food wouldn't all disappear.   The trouble was – I did!

When my Dad turned around to see if I was alright I wasn't there. Highchair and me and my breakfast had skidded to the other end of the dining room and my Dad almost fell over as he came to rescue me.

Anyway, after about five or six

days at sea, we arrived in a place called Halifax and got on a train that was to take us to a big city called Vancouver.

We were on that train for a whole week. We slept on the train and we ate on the train and once we had crossed the prairies we found ourselves travelling through the famous Rocky Mountains.

Of course I don't remember anything about the train journey but it sounds as if it was really exciting.

Maybe someday I will be able to make that same journey again. I would really like that.

Chapter 5 - Please keep going

Our family lived in Vancouver for over a year and that is where one of my brothers was born. The day my Mum had to be taken to the hospital a very nice lady called Mrs. Hay took her in her big car. As they were in a bit of a hurry, even at the railway crossing when the red light was flashing and the gates almost closing to let the train through, Mrs. Hay just went as fast as she could, because my Mum had said to her "keep going Annie!" and the train driver waved his fist at them. Anyway, they got to the hospital just in time.

Eventually, when we were leaving Canada to sail to Japan, it was Mrs. Hay's husband who drove us to Seattle where our ship was waiting for us. This was the first time for me to be in America, although it was just for a day or so.

For some reason our luggage, which consisted of one single bed and two grey metal folding chairs, was put onto the boat at Vancouver but the passengers had to go down to Seattle to embark.

That bed and those two chairs were

all the furniture we owned. But of course in Japan you just sleep and sit on the floor, so it wasn't really a problem.

Chapter 6 – Can you speak Japan?

I was five and a quarter when we arrived in Yokohama. It took us about five days for the 'American Mail' to cross the Pacific Ocean. Actually this was the third ship that I was to sail in so far in my life.

Already I was becoming a bit of a world traveller.

Soon after moving into a little Japanese house, I started kindergarten. On my first day my Mum took me and I just didn't like it at all. I remember kicking the teacher really hard and my Mum just left me there crying and went home. However, I must have settled in because I did enjoy it after that.

Our maid, who wasn't very tall, took me every day. We had to get on two trains to get there. And then after lunch she came back to collect me again.

I think it must have looked as if I was taking her.

If I knew who that teacher was that I kicked I would love to say 'sorry' to her but I'm afraid it's too late now. I do hope her leg got better. That was a terrible thing to do.

Out on the street, well, it wasn't really a street, more a big open space, I played with my Japanese friends every day and that is how I learned how to speak their language. My Mum and Dad had to go to a school to learn it because they were older; but when you are little you just start talking like everyone around you without even thinking about it.

It's what they call 'picking it up'.

- it's the best way to learn a foreign language!

The story behind the title of this chapter came from a visit I made one weekend to a little Sunday school in

33

a town called Ballynahinch – after I returned to Ireland.

I was asked to tell the children about Japan, so I told them how everything was different; like the food, the colour of their hair, the kind of houses they lived in and so on. Then at the end a little boy shot his hand up and asked me in his country accent "but mister can you spaek Japan?"

Chapter 7 – Everybody pull

Where we lived in Tokyo, every year there was a religious festival in honour of the local shrine.

A large brightly coloured float was carried shoulder high through the streets helped along by people pulling on long thick ropes and accompanied by music and dancing.The men had white cloths tied around their heads.

One year my sister and I got into the middle of the procession and when our Dad came looking for us and found us helping to pull it he was very angry and made us come home immediately.

He said that he had come all the way from Ireland to preach against idolatry and his own children were actually helping to pull a heathen idol around the town.

I think it was a bit embarrassing for him but we just thought it was all great fun.

Chapter 8 – a full jeep

One day an American missionary took us on quite a long journey in his jeep. It was what was called a four seater. Well, we all got in: the man and his wife, his little boy and girl, my Mum and my Dad, my sister and my two little brothers and me - and our wee maid Osawa San.

When we were just at the foot of the mountain, beside a river, we found that the bridge had been washed away in a landslide so we had to spend the night in the jeep under a big tree.

My Dad sat in the back on one side

with one of my brothers on each knee; my Mum sat beside him. Then I was curled up on top of one of the back wheel arches – it's like a flat tin plate that covers the wheel - and my sister slept on the other one. The man's wife sat in the front and her two children slept on the driver's seat – the man had to sleep outside on top of the bonnet, or 'the hood', as the Americans called it.

I can't remember where my wee maid went but she didn't need very much room anyway.

The next morning when the bridge was fixed, we started up the long windy mountain road which had 150 very tight and dangerous hairpin bends.

The trains had to go through lots and lots of tunnels and it always took two extra engines at the back to help push them up the mountain.

Chapter 9 – The Waltons

Karuizawa is the name of the town at the very top and it is nice and flat especially for cycling and this is where I learned to ride. My Dad hired two bicycles, one for me and one for my sister; he found a little hill where we got on at the top and he just gave us a big push –I remember ending up in the bushes! And that is how I learned how to ride a bicycle.

Lots of people from Tokyo used to come here in the summer because it is so much cooler. Dotted among the pine trees there were little wooden summer houses everywhere with verandas that would remind you of the kind of house the Waltons lived in.

The town had one long shopping street and there was always a great buzz about it, and you could hear quite a few different European languages as you walked about.

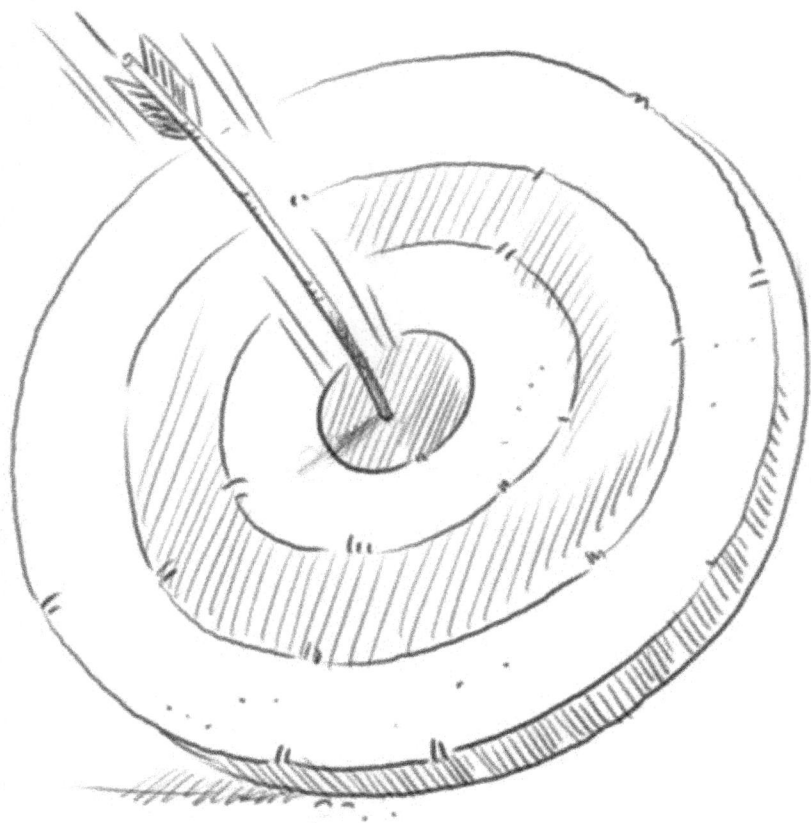

Chapter 10 – the bellybutton

Shibukawa is a small town right in the middle of Japan.   It is still officially called 'the bellybutton of Japan'. We were surrounded by mountains and in the winter the winds were cold and sharp. We lived in a private hospital where the doctor gave us the use of two upstairs rooms and in return my Dad   taught his daughter English. Every morning we were wakened by the radio exercises. It seemed that in every neighbourhood throughout the country and outside many factories people would be doing their warm ups for the day.

A very cheerful lady's voice would be blaring out the instructions to lively piano playing. *"Hai, hajimemasho"* (All right, let's begin)

Outside our window, down in front of the hospital entrance, there was a large square and here our neighbours would gather, all lined up nice and straight, and as soon as the radio started – I think it was at nine o'clock - everyone was doing their daily exercises-

arms up, arms down, legs out, legs in and so on.

It was quite a sight to see , especially in the winter, with the early morning sunshine and people's breath clearly visible against the cold air, and all around us those snow covered mountains that made us feel so safe and secure.

We were the first ever white people to come to live in this valley, so every time we went up the town we were surrounded by crowds of children who kept pointing at us and shouting, "Americans! Americans!" It didn't bother me, but my sister hated it.

We moved from Shibukawa for a time but later came back again when we were able to have our own house.

Chapter 11 – Rabbits, hens and Jip

The name of the town where we lived next was Takasaki. The house was a wee bit out of the town right in the middle of the paddy fields. It was all very flat.The large rambling gardens had a little lake in them and my younger brother and I often tried to make our boat float but it never really worked.

Our so-called boat was the big grey heavy wooden trunk that came with us from Canada and had our Tokyo address painted on it in large black letters.

One day we tried to drown the cat but it got out of the bag and ran away. I had a wee dog called Jip, and we had rabbits and hens as well.

When I was in bed with German measles later at boarding school I had a letter from my Dad to say that Jip had died. It seems that he ate some of the poison that the farmers had put down on the fields for rats.

Sometimes my Dad would kill a hen for our dinner, or 'supper', as it was called. I used to stand and watch him but I don't really think you want to hear the details!

One year we went away on holiday to the foot of Mount Fuji and stayed in a little cabin by the lake. I remember it for two reasons; First of all, it was the only family holiday we ever had while living in Japan, and secondly, I spent the entire week in bed. They told me that I had been suffering from growing pains!?

We had left the rabbits with enough food for seven days but rabbits aren't too bright and instead of eating a wee bit every day, they must have eaten it all the first couple of days, because when we got home they were all dead.

Chapter 12 – Peanut butter and vitamins

When I was seven my Mum and Dad sent me to boarding school in Tokyo. I remember sitting in the school dining hall one day when they were deciding on the school colours; they chose gold and blue. And everyone had a number sewn onto their clothes for the laundry.

The boys' were in blue and the girls' were in red. I was number three and ever since then *three* has been my favourite number and *blue* my favourite colour.

My sister came to my boarding school a year after me and we usually got home once every month but sometimes we went out for the weekend to a very nice American family, the Bergs, who lived in Tokyo. Their three boys were at our school.

At school I played baseball and generally enjoyed everything that was going on.

Miss Ring was the teacher who taught me how to turn a page properly;(you place your right thumb on the page,lift the top right corner towards you with the index finger and slowly slide your hand downwards) My Dad used to say that if I never learnt anything else at school, at least I now knew how to turn a page properly.

Miss Ring was tall and thin and had a very nice smile.

My dormitory master was called Mr James. He was very kind to all of the boys.

Every two weeks or so all the boys were walked in single file through the narrow country lanes to the local village where we all had our hair cut.

And every morning there was inspection; We had to be up, washed, dressed and standing at the end of our bunks with our arms stretched out, and Mr James always checked behind our ears as well.

Often on Saturdays, my friends and

I would take a picnic and go along the railway line for about a mile or so. It was great fun. We stayed out all day.

My favourite sandwiches were peanut butter. You just had to go to the dining hall and the lady would make you whatever you wanted.

Chapter 13   Dad! my shoe

I remember feeling quite sad sometimes when my Dad and Mum left us back to school after being home because I knew that my Dad didn't have enough money for the train fare home and it was over 100 miles away.

But they always seemed to get home all right – I guess God looked after them.

But still it was always quite sad to see them walking away from the school gates to the local train station.

Talking about the trains in Tokyo, on one trip with my family, we were so crushed and pushed around that at a station where we 'didn't' want to get off, I got shoved towards the door and lost one of my shoes. We had to get off at the next station and get a train back again. My shoe was down on the track and we were able to rescue it and continue our journey.

But it was always exciting when we were able to get up home on a weekend from school.

At school, every morning all the American pupils brought their jars of vitamins with them to breakfast and they also stuck their chewing gum under the table and then after breakfast they put it back in their mouths. No wonder they needed to take vitamins. I remember thinking, 'what a filthy habit!'

Funny, that's something I never did – vitamins or chewing gum.

Chapter 14 The big shiny face

Mrs Best, the headmaster's wife made the most delicious meatloaf. We had it quite often along with spinach and I just loved it. I think it was my favourite meal.

Our maid at Takasaki was a very good cook too and I loved the way she made scrambled eggs in the frying pan and then sliced it into triangles like a cake.

I think Mrs Beckon, the American missionary who was there before us, taught her to cook.

This is a different maid from the one that took me to kindergarten.

She was tall for a Japanese and had a broad shiny face, and always smiling.

I found out that she put on a lot of Pond's cold cream every day. She was very kind to our family and we loved her.

I suppose she was just like our big sister. Her name was Michiko San.

It was in this big rambling house in Takasaki that one day we found, up in the attic, what just looked like a long box. Actually it was what was called a box organ.

You unfolded it until it just sat there like an old-fashioned pedal organ.

Well, that's how I learned to play – I just hit the notes until they sounded right.

Chapter 15 -Dinky toy or cardigan?

Sometimes the postman would arrive with a parcel from Ireland, America, Canada or some other country and my Mum and Dad used to search through all of their coat pockets looking for the sixty yen you had to pay to the postman before he could leave it.

There were many times when we four children went to the window and watched him taking the parcel away again. These mainly contained food that could not be purchased in Japan. I remember once a parcel arriving and the loose tea and the tin of treacle had burst open making the entire contents virtually unusable.

But I also remember that in one parcel there was a lovely blue sleeveless cardigan that had been hand knitted especially for me and I wore it almost every day until I was just too big for it. It was my favourite present and I wish I knew the lady who sent it to me so that I could thank her for it.

One year I got a dinky toy but the cardigan was my favourite.

Oh yes, and in that same parcel there was a bar of Cadbury's Dairy

Milk Chocolate all for me. I don't know if my sister and brothers got one as well; they certainly never shared any of it and I suppose I didn't give them any of mine.

I used to take it out into the middle of the paddy fields and sitting against a haystack slowly eat one wee square. Then I would fold it all up again carefully and eat another square the next week. I think the bar lasted me about three months.

It was five years before I got another one.

The road in front of our house was dry and dusty, especially when buses went past. Dust just covered the whole place. It seemed to come in big grey clouds. Although the nearest bus stop was down the road where we had to go for our drinking water, they always used to stop at our door to let us on or off.

My Dad had to take containers on a flat cart which he hitched onto his bicycle and hand pumped the water up from the well. We used to run along side to make sure the containers didn't fall over.

The bus drivers and conductors were all very friendly. There was one very nice conductor who used to come to our church and it was always great to get onto her bus.

She was great fun and always had a big smile for us. These lady conductors were always very polite and would apologise for even the slightest delay at a traffic light or a left or right hand turn.

Even when the bus arrived at the station 'on the dot' they would apologise to the passengers for being late.

Chapter 16- I salute you

One day, when I was eight or nine, the whole school was taken to the big airport in Tokyo to hear a famous American preacher; his name was Billy Graham. I don't remember anything he said but he stood on a box in one corner of the airport lounge and he was wearing a white raincoat with the collar standing up.

I didn't really know anything about him at the time but later on when I was older I discovered what a great man he was and have admired him ever since.

Every morning in class we had to do what was called the 'Pledge of Allegiance'. The American flag - it was called 'the stars and stripes' - was at the front of the room and you had to put one hand on your heart and recite it together.

"I pledge allegiance to the flag of the United States of America and to the Republic for which it stands: one Nation under God, indivisible, with Liberty and Justice for all."

This was most interesting because only half of the class was American. But it taught you to respect other cultures and in any case most of us, I think, felt that we were citizens of the world.

Chapter 17 – the fancy shirt!

I remember having two friends come to our house at Takasaki one summer for a holiday. Their parents were missionaries too. They were brother and sister and were about the same age as my sister and me.

The thing is, Ron wore one of those really smart Canadian shirts with squares, like the loggers wear – you see them in the movies; they felt soft and flannelly and, well, I never had any fancy clothes.

It was in different shades of green.

It's a bit embarrassing now but I must have talked so much about his shirt the whole time they were there that after they'd gone I found it wrapped up in brown paper in a drawer as a present for me.

I felt so ashamed that I never wore it.

I just couldn't.

Chapter 18 – all alone in Tokyo

One year during the summer holidays when we were all at home together, my Dad needed to go to the bank in Tokyo to cash a cheque but he didn't have enough money for a full adult train fare. But as he had enough for a half fare I had to go for him. It took three and a half hours from Shibukawa to Ueno, a very large station close to Tokyo where trains came in from all over the country, like a hub, you could say. And then from there I had to change twice to get onto the central loop line that took you to Tokyo Central station. Once I got out at Tokyo I had to walk two or three blocks. The crowds were pressing in all around me and I was terrified of being carried off in the wrong direction so I stayed close to the big grey buildings, holding on to them, until I arrived at the Hongkong and Shanghai Banking Corporation. I stood and looked up at it for a minute and then went inside and asked for the manager. The counter seemed very high – but you see I was just eleven and a half and at that time I wasn't all that tall.

Once I had done the business I had

to remember how to get back again to Ueno station, where I went into one of the station restaurants and had a curry while waiting for my train.

I suppose it was 10 o'clock at night before I got back to Shibukawa where Dad was waiting for me outside the station with our old grey Willys Overland jeep. When it wouldn't start, Mum used to say that it gave her the Willys!

But Dad, who was very patient about such things simply prayed about it, and that usually did the trick.

Something we always looked forward to when travelling by train was the 'eki bento' (station lunches)

Sellers would walk up and down the platform with various snacks and drinks in a large basket hanging down in front of them from their shoulders and from it you could make a purchase through the train window.

One of the most famous stations for delicious 'ekiben' was Takasaki and passengers would often wait until they reached that particular station before buying their lunches. The hot green tea which came in quaint little square china teapots with wire handles was very refreshing especially in hot weather. The little china lid was your cup.

The lunch usually consisted of 'sushi' – little rice cakes wrapped in sheets of dried seaweed with various vegetables in the centre. And with it there was always the various pickles, like cucumbers, plums, radishes and red ginger thinly sliced.

As well as not taking too many cold drinks, another thing that we learned not to do in the summer was to continually fan yourself – it just made you worse.

Of course, if there was an electric fan close by that was all right, because it was doing all the work for you and you could sit still and enjoy the cool breeze.

Chapter 19 - The last biscuit

Because it was just after the second world war, certain foods were still scarce in Japan and one of them was milk, but we were able to get powdered milk from the Australian Army Base in Tokyo and there is a story about the tin.

My Mum kept biscuits in one of them once the milk powder was all used up, and around the opening was a very sharp edge.

One day my brother and I stuck our hands in at the same time to try and get the last biscuit; well, we both cut our wrists and have stitches in exactly the same place to prove it!

We were rushed to the doctor's and the last biscuit stayed in the tin.

Chapter 20 – A red bicycle

When I was twelve our family went back to Ireland for a holiday and I had to go to a primary school in Belfast. It was called Harding Memorial.

I made a really good friend at this school; his name was Victor Cardoo who was born in Nigeria to missionary parents. We used to go out for a walk on our lunch break. I remember thinking that he was very different from the rest of the boys being a keen christian and serious minded.

Most weekends when Dad had to preach somewhere the whole family went with him and when we were at different people's houses for tea we were always asked to sing in Japanese. (Dad had composed quite a number of tunes to Japanese bible verses.) And after we sang the man in the house would give us half a crown, which in today's money is twelve and a half pence.

One song we loved singing a lot is:

"Mazu Kami no kuni to Kami no gi to o motomeyo; saraba subete koreranomono wa warerani kuwaeraru beshi"

(See ye first the Kingdom of God ...)

We were in Ireland for a year and a half and in that time I had saved enough money to buy a new bicycle to take back to Japan.

In fact, we had six new bicycles to go back with us.

Mine was a Raleigh and it was bright red and it cost me fourteen pounds and ten shillings.

One Sunday after a meeting in a place called Broughshane where my Dad had preached, I said to him in the car going home that I didn't think he had got on very well and my Mum was very cross with me for saying that. She didn't want to hurt his feelings.

But I think it was just that he had

got out of the way of preaching in English.

Chapter 21 – .. and just who is Bobbie?

Back in Japan my Dad started to teach us at home but I'm afraid it didn't work very well for me, so I was then sent to the local Japanese high school which I enjoyed very much. I made great friends there. The name of the school was Shibukawa Kougyo Kooto Gakko.

We had to wear a special uniform in which you could be mistaken for a Salvation Army officer. It was black with gold buttons and had a very tight stand up collar. All the boys had to have their heads shaved. Thankfully the headmaster allowed me to keep my hair on but I did wear the uniform which was actually quite smart on me, although I say it myself.

Another thing that I discovered on returning to Shibukawa from Ireland was that there had arrived what you could call ' a new kid on the block' and I have to be honest when I tell you that I was not best pleased – a bit jealous, I'm afraid. You see, before, it was all "Burukku chan, Burukku chan" and now all I could hear was "Babbi chan, Babbi chan".

Yes, Bobby Vermay's parents were American missionaries who had arrived during our absence and Bobby had become very popular with the townsfolk.

When I found out where he lived, I went to meet him and right away we became good friends.

He was no threat at all!

We used to go out into the villages together on our bikes with a picnic lunch and gather the children for a meeting on a grassy patch. We taught them choruses and told them bible stories. I think Bobby was a couple of years younger than me – he was certainly a bit shorter than I was.

Chapter 22 – My new scooter

When I was 14, my Dad took me down the town in Shibukawa and bought me a brand new scooter. It was called a Pigeon and it was white and grey: I just loved that scooter and the beauty of it was that in those days you didn't need to wear any protective wear, like a helmet or anything – you were free!

Every day I went to the shops for my Mum on my scooter. I went to the butcher's and the baker's and the vegetable shop where often I helped serve the customers. The local shopkeepers were very special friends of mine and I enjoyed being with them.

Everyone in Shibukawa knew me on my scooter. They used to call out my name and wave as I whizzed past.

Unfortunately you weren't allowed to take your scooter to school. The day after I got it, obviously wanting my friends to see it, I took my younger brother on the back so that he could ride it home again for me.

I think he must have either been going too fast or hit a stone, because he came off it on his way back, and all down one side of my new scooter was all scraped and damaged.

But I didn't say anything to him – he was annoyed and that was enough. We got it fixed and nothing more was said about it.

I used to go to a town about an hour from Shibukawa called Nakanojo every Sunday evening to help with a meeting, because my Dad had a service in Shibukawa at the same time.

And on another evening I would go up to Ikaho, a well known spa town, to take what was called a cottage meeting for my Dad as well. A spa is where hot water springs up through the rocks and the sulphur in it has healing qualities. People travel from far and wide to get relief from all kinds of pains.

In the winter I went by bus but in the summer I went on my scooter.

The very first time I preached I was 14 and I talked about Moses and the snakes.

My text sounded like this:

"Mose ga arano de hebi o ageta yoni, Hitonoko mo onajiyoni agerarenakereba naranai".

Chapter 23 - Baptisms

Another very important thing that happened to me when I was 14 is that I was baptised. Well, it didn't just happen. I decided I wanted to be baptized. In Japan, it takes the people so long to really understand the meaning of the christian message, that only when it becomes very clear to them, and they are able to make a decision to become followers of Jesus Christ, do they get baptized to mark the date. I guess it must have been the same for me. My friend Jimmy baptized me along with some others in the Tone river that runs past the town.

Jimmy isn't his real name. It is Kitano but he was called Jimmy when he worked at the American Army Base, and after that all he got in our house was Jimmy.

After the baptisms we had communion on the shore; we just sat down on the stones. Then when that was over we all had a picnic. It was always a very special time for the church.

Another very amusing thing often happened at baptisms.

Because the Japanese are so modest, four of the older ladies from the church would make a kind of wind shield with blankets, and they would hold the four corners while the preacher got changed in order to give him some privacy.

The thing is, they always stood inside!

But that's Japan.

Chapter 24 – Home James!

When I was attending the local Japanese High School, during English classes the teacher used to sit at my desk while I stood at the front telling everyone how to pronounce the words properly.   The teacher was a very nice man but he was quite embarrassed because his English was poor. I tried not to make him feel too bad!

When I was about 15   I went to different people's houses to teach their children English – one family used to send their chauffeur to pick me up and take me home again.

I had to sit in the back and it made me feel quite important . . . . . and no, I didn't wave!

One family that was special to me was called Machida. I taught their eldest son English. His father was a very kind man and he let me drive his car sometimes up at the school grounds. His wife's father was the mayor of Shibukawa when we were there. He was tall for a Japanese and looked quite European and very striking as he walked up and down the main street of the town.

I forgot to tell you about another lovely wee village I went to, I think twice a month, to have a children's meeting. I went by bus because the roads were very rough and stony. It was a hot spring tucked away in the mountains. I stayed overnight at the local inn, where I would enjoy a hot bath, sleep on the straw matted floor on a 'futon' and then in the morning, after the traditional breakfast of soup, rice and roasted mackerel or herring, catch the first bus out to Nakanojo, where I would change buses for Shibukawa.

For me this was the real Japan – untouched by the western lifestyle that could now been seen in many of the large cities up and down the country.

The place was called Sawatari and although I never saw any myself, the locals claimed that wild foxes could often be seen in those mountains.

Chapter 25 – ... and don't come back

Another thing that happened in Shibukawa is that I was sent to music.

The teacher was a quaint old lady who lived alone, except for all her little yappy dogs. She treated them like babies and some even had nappies on them! And she had a very loud voice that sounded just like one of her dogs barking.

Well, after just one year she told me not to come back and all I was doing wrong was playing twice as many notes as there were on the sheet, because

I thought it sounded better.

And it did!

In any case, being able to play the piano mostly by ear later proved very useful. I always wondered why I was invited to all the parties.

Chapter 26 – The Russian musician

In the summer my Dad used to have special gospel missions in a tent near a canal that ran down through the centre of the town.

We drove around the streets with posters advertising the meetings and used a loud speaker to draw people's attention.

I sometimes played the organ in the tent and there was a young Japanese man who played the violin. His proper name was Horigome Makoto but he told everyone that it was Horigomento Makowski. I think he imagined himself as a famous Russian musician or something. He was a wee bit strange, but harmless enough – smiled a lot and seemed to talked to himself.

And there was a Japanese lady who used to sing a solo - she fancied herself as an opera singer, the way she posed and smiled and performed and all that.

But she was actually a very hearty person and a good friend of our family. The Japanese love singing and performing in public.

My best friend was called Hiro. He was great fun and you should have seen him on *his* scooter!

He used to sit facing backwards and with his arms stretched behind him, ride down through the town.

The policeman who stood at the corner was not too pleased, and would blow his whistle at him as he often did at me when I used to ride my bicycle down past him, swerving and with no hands.

The things you do when you are young and fearless!

Chapter 27 – My very own passport

I remember when I was sixteen being taken by my Dad to see Mr Pickles, the British Consul in Tokyo to get my very own passport. I was so proud of it that all the way home in the train I kept reading what it said on the inside cover.

It told me that the Queen of England promised to protect me wherever I went in the world and that no one would dare to stop or hinder me.

I didn't realize it at the time but this was in preparation for my sister and me being sent back to Ireland. I don't really know why we were sent back because I loved living in Japan. I loved the place, I loved the people, I loved the food and I loved helping my Dad with his work.

Anyway, sure if I hadn't come to Ireland, I would never have met you two wonderful girls!!

Remind me to let you see that passport some day.

Chapter 28 – Ship ahoy!

As our big ship, the 'Chusan', began to sail away from the pier at Yokohama we could see our Mum and Dad and our two wee brothers and Ronnie Cairns, and I suppose others, standing on the quay holding the other end of our streamers. In fact everyone on the ship held a paper ribbon and their friends who were standing on the shore held the other end of it.

The band played , the ship's horn gave a loud blast, and as we moved slowly away, one by one the streamers began to snap until soon they were all in the water and our family and friends got smaller and smaller until they and Japan were soon completely out of sight.

Chapter 29 – Just one egg

I should have told you a story about Ronnie Cairns; I visited him one day in his Tokyo flat and as he was a bachelor at the time and didn't have much practice at cooking, he didn't know what to make us for lunch. I asked him, "what have you got?" and he said that he had just one egg and all he could do was to boil it.Well, I had a bit more experience in cooking so I suggested that we scramble it! I think he was quite impressed and years later we used to talk and laugh about the scrambled egg.

Chapter 30 – What a lady!

It took us 4 days to sail to Hong Kong. There we were met by very special friends of our family.

They lived in an apartment high up on a hill and at night we could see the 'Chusan' out in the middle of Hong Kong harbour all beautifully lit up and glittering in the moonlight. It was quite a sight.

Mrs. Milliken was tall and elegant and as I recall, wore lovely, long, flowing dresses. I remember one was pale blue and she wore it with the collar standing up. She took us one day to their club for club sandwiches and lemonade – it was the first time we had ever had anything like that.

Well, I didn't say it to anyone at the time but I decided that one day I would marry a classy lady like Mrs. Milliken

...............and I did.

Chapter 31 You almost missed the boat, Madam

Singapore was our next stop, where we left the ship as it sailed up the coast to Penang.   Friends took us up inland through Malaya, and then getting on the boat again at Penang we sailed to Colombo which is now called Sri Lanka.

Because the harbour there wasn't deep enough, our ship had to lie out in the bay and launches took us ashore.

We didn't have very long there; I think just an afternoon, so you had to watch your time. Well, when the ship was steaming away from Colombo, all of a sudden this launch came flying through the water with its hooter going and the pilot waving like mad. One of our passengers, a lady, had missed the boat, so our ship had to stop and a long rope ladder was thrown down the side of the ship for her to climb up on.

On Sundays on the ship I had a little Sunday School and used the piano that was in the band stand to teach the children some choruses.

The next stop was Bombay. It was really amazing to see children on the pier waiting for people on the ship to throw coins into the water. They were able to see if the money was any value to them as it glided through the air and they only went in after it if it was.

They must have had great eyesight. Maybe they ate a lot of carrots!

Chapter 32 – The Egyptian Dressing gown

From Aden we sailed through the Suez Canal to Port Said where men came on board to sell us all sorts of local souvenirs and items of clothing. I bought my Dad a blue dressing gown made from Egyptian cotton, and when we got to Naples I went ashore and posted it at a local post office. Unfortunately my Dad didn't get it for about three months.

I discovered that the man in the post office made me pay for airmail but sent it by sea. When I talked later to friends who lived in Italy, I found that this sort of thing is quite common.

It's still not very nice and it is definitely dishonest.

Chapter 33 – A Mediterranean Cruise

I think our last port of call was Las Palmas in the Canaries. We bought a pineapple and when we got back to our cabin, we sliced it and ate it.

I think this was the first time I ever tasted a real pineapple.

One of the things I loved was that at every port, just before the ship was about to sail, a band of around a dozen or so men would be on the pier in their smart white uniforms with white helmets. They would play really lively and jolly tunes, such as 'Colonel

Bogey', but sometimes even sad songs like 'We'll meet again, don't know where, don't know when; but I know we'll meet again some sunny day' and people would be crying and waving at those they were leaving behind- and the atmosphere and emotion was wild! I loved it.

The other thing was the uniforms that the officers and stewards all wore on the ship.

They were all dressed in white until a certain date, when all of a sudden overnight they would appear in black.

It depended on the time of year.

Summer or winter, the passengers spent most of their time out on deck.

In the winter we were brought beef tea which was very nourishing and warmed you up inside;

In summer it was always ice cream.

The food was as good as you would get in any top class French restaurant and the variety was certainly better than we had ever seen. It was sheer luxury.

'The Peninsular and Oriental Steam Navigation Company' certainly did it with style.

Curled up in a deck chair, I would spend the entire day just looking out at the sea and the horizon beyond - dreaming - yes, dreaming of the wonderful life I had now left behind me and wondering, just wondering, what lay ahead.

Very soon our ship would slowly be steaming its way up through the English Channel and into London's famous Tilbury Docks where at last we would have to say good-bye to our big floating hotel, that had brought us safely from the other side of the world.

Chapter 34 – The missing ticket

Oh! I forgot to tell you that our tickets were to take us just to London because there wasn't enough money to buy them for the whole journey to Belfast. Dad had asked us if we believed God would provide for the rest of the journey and we said we did.

Our uncles and aunts were waiting for us in Ireland and needed to know what boat we were coming on from London because in those days that was the way most people crossed the Irish Sea.

Only famous people or those with plenty of money could fly.

Well, the thing is, as we passed through all of those countries, and met different people who knew our Dad, some of them gave us little gifts of money.

When we phoned our aunt and uncle from London we told them that we were flying home! They were really surprised and of course, we were really proud of ourselves. We wouldn't have called the king our uncle!

The whole journey took us five weeks.

My sister went to live with Aunt Jean and Uncle Joe, and I went to live with my Mum's older sister Aunt Hannah and her husband Uncle Tom. And there we were well looked after for the next ten months until our Mum and Dad and two brothers joined us.

I didn't know it then, but a year later, still only eighteen, I would be left to look after my three younger siblings while our parents would return to their work in Japan, and we wouldn't see them again for another four years.

Chapter 35 – What a poser!

The very first thing I did when I got to Belfast was, and you might think it a bit odd or even a bit conceited, I bought myself a green tweed suit and went down to the photographic studios in Belfast and had my portrait taken. I was seventeen.

I remembered seeing a portrait of my mother when she was eighteen and also of other people. It seemed to me that it was what people used to do and, I suppose, at that age, you do look young and fresh with a sparkle in your eyes. Everyone should have their portrait taken when they are seventeen or eighteen.

I'm sure you have seen the picture. It's on the hall table in our house.

And now when Nana gets me to dust the table with all the photographs, I make sure that yours Alex is on my left and that yours Faye is on my right - just where you always liked to be.

Well, girls, there you are now!

These are some stories for you to tell your grandchildren one day.

Thank you for listening.

With all my love

Grandpa

xx

'Timber Cottage' Carrowdore - 5th April 2009

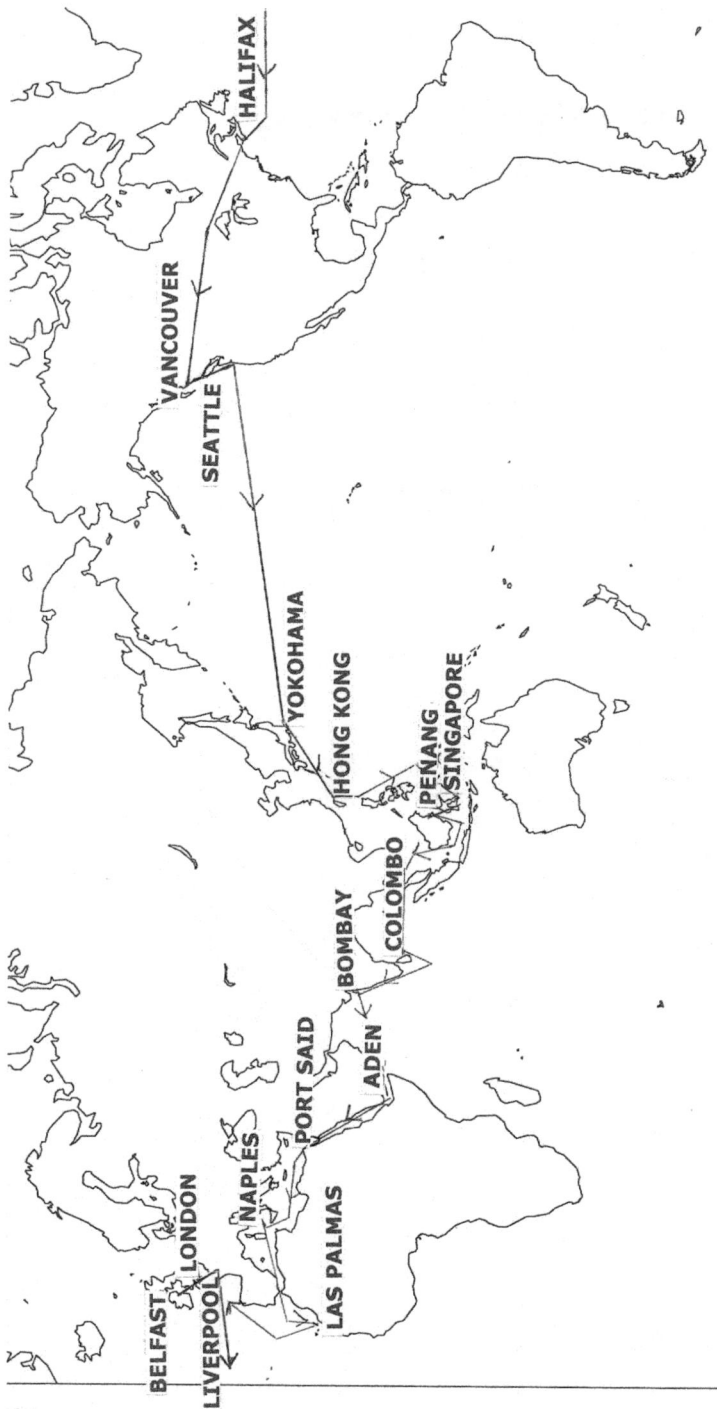

HALIFAX

VANCOUVER

SEATTLE

YOKOHAMA

HONG KONG

PENANG
SINGAPORE

BOMBAY

COLOMBO

PORT SAID

ADEN

NAPLES

LAS PALMAS

BELFAST
LONDON
LIVERPOOL

TAKASAKI

SAWATARI
NAKANOJO

IKAHO
KARUIZAWA   SHIBUKAWA

UENO
MOUNT FUJI   TOKYO

Lightning Source UK Ltd.
Milton Keynes UK
UKHW010655300920
370782UK00001B/31

9 781438 994482